Hollie Jean Huff was born in Alaska but moved before forming much memory of the place. She loves ballet, gardening, snow, reading, and, in spite of being an adult, toy animals. She has a strong interest in some of the history before the time of photographs. Two reasons why she wrote this book are that: one, she focuses on trying even when life is hard but also tries to know when to quit, and two, she had a hard time finding good books to read so she wrote one of her own.

Hollie Jean Huff

WEAK LOVE AND STRONG LOVE

Chapter 1
Wilted

A flighty, good-looking, terrible man had tried to cheat on his wife in Russia – tried and failed. He was fairly good at lying. Bitterness was a disease in his house. This is a story about wilted, ignored love and beautiful, lasting love. A holy book tells us, "To sin is to earn death." Many who are too proud try to tell themselves they will escape this rule and that there are many ways to do so, but the truth remains. No one escapes this law. This latest fool was a father of four children still alive and one dead child. He was also a husband of a serious, shrewd wife a few years older than him. He had a serious and very important job. This annoying man was toying about in his mind how he could get away with what he had done and/or solve the problem, and he did not focus much on the fact that these two goals were contradictory. He usually enjoyed life and did not care that much if other people did or not. It sometimes took other people a while to realize how selfish he was because he tended to pay a lot of attention to others if he found them interesting, and he was generous with gifts and offerings from his soul. But that soul was shallow. He usually got what he wanted, and it had always been this way for him.

His name was Alexei Romovsky, and true love was eluding him at this point in his life. It usually had. It did that to all men of his type, but he didn't think about that. He believed it would probably come back, and this put him in a good mood. He was not an extremely realistic man. Romovsky's wife was a very realistic woman. She hated being lied to, and her husband had lied to her. She hated a lot of things. She hated the girl who had been the object of her husband's affections. She hated the confrontations with him but could not resist them. She hated her wrinkles, rainy weather, wilted flowers, awkward social situations, the fact that not all her offspring had lived, and so on. It was a long list. She liked to dwell on it.

These confrontations between the husband and wife were very stormy. Usually, he came to her and tried to plead for forgiveness with eloquent words and quiet charm. Her response was to scream, cry, and use words with such rage and venom that he recoiled with horror, shock, and even a little fear. She called him names she'd never called him before. She felt such strong self-pity. He had horrible timing. He had never been afraid of his wife before. He was confused by this new feeling.

The children of this broken couple still married were disillusioned children who had lost what little respect and love they had felt for their father. The household was in danger of turning into a mess. The staff was disgusted. The children were still so young. The oldest was seven years old. Though they cared little for their mother, they respected her more than their father.

So, someone planned to try to visit and perhaps help fix this unholy mess.

It had been no good way to honor and mourn his dead child by trying to cheat on his wife with one of the very pretty girls who were not in his social class. So, this mess would be very hard to fix. The wife's name was Maria. The friend of the family (such as it was at this time) who was coming to visit was Katerina Anastova. Anastova was a very pretty, intelligent, but emotionally charged woman. She was going to try to help this vain, muddled man stay with his family, for that was what she had decided he must do. It was anyone's guess if it would work. And the husband, at least, had not been stupid enough to defend his actions in front of his wife. The husband did not have much faith in Anastova's ability to heal the rift. He was too deep in sadness and the hopelessness of his sin. He tried to think more of why he had done it, for he did not fully know.

The friends of this man were all morally somewhat vague and tended to survive more on luck and favoritism than ability. None of them were geniuses. The husband of Maria had thought it wouldn't do to have friends who were too smart. He and his friends were all more or less alike. They did not take life too seriously. They did not notice all the mistakes they made or feelings they hurt.

Katerina had a big job ahead of her.

She stayed with this family for one week and witnessed several heated scenes between the married couple. The wife screamed so harshly; Katerina was afraid the woman would lose her voice. The wife even slapped her mate's face, though she was not a very strong woman. She still felt she was making her point. It was not usual for Russian nobles to slap one another, but the wife did it anyway. She was past the point of caring. He was not acting like a prince, except that he did not slap her back. He had never hit a woman or a little girl. He became very attentive to his children.

Young Katerina managed to work out an imperfect reconciliation between the couple whose love had wilted and died. She listened to them both separately and together and then coached the man for his apologies. She was friendly and playful to the children. She was almost overly polite to the servants. She wanted attention so badly that it was easy to be almost too nice.

"I thank you for coming to rescue me from the wrath of my wife and helping to heal the broken glass that was my marriage."

"It would have healed with or without me." But he shook his head.

"I'm not as sure of that as you are. Go home and rest."

He helped her into the carriage himself rather than having someone else do it whether that was the way it was customary or not. There were more social rules for upper-class Russians than for some of the other nobilities, but Romovsky was very happy and wanted to help her himself. He patted the horse, as he was not afraid of horses, and told the coachman to be careful. At this time, the slightly melted-back-together marriage had more to do with the husband's begging than Katerina's help, but Romovsky was grateful for her intervention, as he had been so afraid to keep approaching his wife by himself. He smiled at Katerina. She was off to catch a train.

Chapter 2
Tense Dinner

Romovsky knew a man named Vladimir Oblesky. He did not know him very well. They were to have dinner together that evening. Romovsky did not recall very well the reason for meeting. The restaurant was fancy, of course. It took a lot of money to have a tense dinner. The lovely glow of gaslights giving the false illusion of smoke would shine on chandeliers and plush chairs. These two men did not like each other but behaved in a relatively friendly manner to each other, as was the custom. The reason they were dining together was that Vladimir was interested in being the husband of a family member of Romovsky, and Vladimir wanted to discuss it with him against his own will. Vladimir found it hard to discuss anything personal with this man. Vladimir was a rich farmer who had to travel to Moscow for this dinner. These men were nobility, not royalty.

"The war at home is over. The wife is no longer boiling over about that girl. I don't see why she was so very upset, as I'd failed at obtaining my desire," Romovsky told his nervous dinner companion. He was partly joking.

"I'm here to discuss something serious with you and not to hear more about your blizzard of a family," Vladimir half-joked back.

This dinner, at which too much food was served, helped him decide, by watching Romovsky closely, how he should proceed with Natalia.

He was very nervous about proposing and not just because he was the kind of man who got so nervous about a woman he liked. He almost felt like falling through the ice into the river rather than asking for wedlock. He had another very bitter reason. Romovsky had let him know in his charming, yet tactless, way that the farmer still had competition for this girl as far as making her a wife. A noble military man named Sergei Shermetov had been courting her for a very few weeks. Natalia loved him in a half-blind, yet hard to understand, way. Vladimir had known this. He stubbornly hoped he had a chance because he felt it was not entirely wise for her to love this young man from out of town. He also felt he had more of a chance to wed her than she knew because he had learned Shermetov was not telling her he had been with several women not of the pure sort before he began to solely court her. He had engaged in several other less-than-puritanical habits with some of his army fellows. In short, his morals had always been full of holes. The morals of Sergei's parents had been no better. They had been unfaithful to each other and the church while spending a fortune on nothing. Vladimir knew he took his own sins much more seriously, even to the point of having dark religious feelings about them as far as he understood religion. He had not had a romantic liaison, bad or otherwise, with a woman before. He knew this would rank high on her list of priorities if she had known these facts. Vladimir hoped Natalia's purity would save her from more folly. It upset him that a woman he loved was enough of a fool, though she was smart and emotional, to risk her heart on this good-looking devil with fake angel wings. It confused him.

Chapter 3
Yes and No

On his way to Princess Natalia's residence, Vladimir was working on his conscience and on his courage. It did not seem to Vladimir that Shermetov was complicated enough to keep Natalia's affections for life. Did she not see this? The answer must lie with Shermetov's ability to lie and distract people from the facts; this he could do, as he had the manners of a noble but not the heart. He knew Shermetov really loved Natalia but loving her was easy. What would he do if life got hard? Vladimir did not doubt Natalia's basic purity and wisdom and knew there was no way she had surrendered herself completely to this man. Vladimir could not have loved her otherwise, nor could any other man.

Natalia was at home.

She had been thrilled with her great success in society. So much about her was praised. Sincerely and insincerely, her dancing was praised for its delicate elegance and emphasis on femininity. Her beauty gained many comments, of course. She was tall, with long, dark hair, grey/blue eyes, and a slim build. She carried her height well. Her graceful motions were obvious even when she was just walking. She was not boring even when she was still. Her thoughts and feelings came and went very fast.

When the hall porter opened the door for Vladimir on this day of nerves, she was scared. The problem was not that she had any great disgust because of this man. She liked him a little but did not love him in a romantic sense. She had fears about being ready to be wed, no matter who the groom was. She liked to be admired; she knew he admired her a great deal. So, he had a powerful effect on her. He did not talk much. She valued conversation a great deal. She felt that if he added more to his personality, perhaps he would be a good husband for some other woman but not her.

She tried to seem composed. He tried to be formal. He had in his mind the firm decision to make this short. He paused in front of her and went paler. When he looked at her face, he shocked them both with what he said. In a quiet voice, he said, "I came here thinking of marriage, but the time is wrong. I was wrong."

Some of the light faded from her eyes. She was flattered. Her soul sparkled because she loved flattery so much. It had many times brought tears to her eyes. But she had to sort out the feelings of the man before her. She loved another man so much. She was almost always blind to his many shortcomings. His charm was so strong. It seemed to cover the frost in his soul. The fear she sometimes suffered in her beloved's presence and also when he was gone was unexplainable to her. She did not see it was her mind trying to talk to her heart so as to let her know he was not the man for her. She did not see he had weaknesses because he had courage when it came to physical fights and enduring the pain they could cause. Also, he was so witty. He had always been able to attract any woman he flirted with. If she had known this, she would have been sick in body and soul. Her lover was not man enough to handle an innocent, youthful woman who did not know a great deal about men or marital matters. He needed something or someone used because his soul was so pathetic in its baseness that he could not organize his thoughts well enough to keep a decent woman happy. He needed a pretty woman in his life, but it did not matter to him very much which pretty woman it was. She did not know what she took for firmness in his character was truly a cruel stubbornness. His greatest desires had to do with his career. He was very aware of the way other men saw him. Like some other men almost since the beginning of time, he thought more of himself than others. He had tried to convince himself this made perfect sense and was all very well because so many other men did it, including males in high positions of power. He lacked the religious education and depth of soul to see into the future so as to tell what the consequences of one's loves and actions would be. He had seen women he had pursued romantic affairs with as sources of pleasure more than whole people. He had proved so faithful to Natalia in word and deed, and the beauty of this was part of what had fooled her. Her mother liked him a little; her father did not. The father believed Sergei should have been drowned in Moscow's river. He knew the young man was a cruel, spiteful, and an overly proud liar. The father feared very much for his daughter's reputation as well as her heart. The mother loved her daughter but did not always see through the seemingly sweet attention she was being shown as a potential future-mother-in-law. She had argued with her husband so many times for years. She was now desensitized to listening to him on important matters. Her Russian mind was, however, lacking full trust in a man who was a little less attentive to her daughter than he should have been. She had noticed Sergei looking coldly at her daughter's eyes.

The Romovsky family did not communicate within itself very well.

Natalia let the man before her know she was stunned by letting her mouth hang open in silence. She felt uncertain, so she also let him know she could not predict the future. The way she said this put some vague hope in him that maybe she would wed him later. Her heart felt two things at once, and this gave her such despair.

His face had become so stiff. Then, he shocked her more by saying a very personal thing, "Do NOT marry HIM." A seed had been planted. He bowed to her and left, leaving was what he wanted. She had been obviously confused, so he was confused too. He did not wish to be in that house leaving himself at risk of seeing other people he knew (some of them being members of her family). He wanted to feel the cold air. He wanted to stay alone in a hotel for the night and then go to his home in the country.

During this time in Russia in the late 1800s, one of the most healing things was to be alone for a while. This applied to peasants and nobility alike. It was one of the few traits they shared.

Chapter 4
Love's Mistake

There was a very strong social rule among the Russian nobles that if someone was about to make a huge mistake in their personal life, they must face the bad results because no one was supposed to tell them they were about to make a mistake beforehand. If the sufferer was stupid enough to fail to begin with, there was no help for it.

Natalia's mother longed to disobey this rule and warn her daughter of the fear that gripped her maternal heart and grew. So much was on the mother's mind, but she never forgot her daughter.

The mother began the conversation she wanted to have and yet did not wish to have.

"I want to see you happy. I want to like this man, but my heart is in halves. For some reasons I cannot name, I fear he is not the right mate of life for you."

The daughter did not know what to say, so she stayed silent for a few moments. She was stunned, hurt, relieved, and very, very stressed. She stared at her mother. Finally, the daughter in distress gave her mother a weak smile. She began to speak French.

"I know you speak out of fear for my future. When love rules too much, the mind will be afraid."

The mother wished to speak again. She loved her daughter enough. She was willing to let this mysterious courtship from Shermetov come to an end to save her daughter's soul. She was willing to let it all stop and let society be confused if it would spare her offspring from disaster. It was a high price she was willing to pay.

"You are one of the only people I've ever loved. I remember you so well when you were a little girl."

Natalia burst into tears. So many emotions welled up in her. They came out in sobs and gasps. Her mind would not come up with the words to explain her love for her mother but also for the man it hurt so much to lose faith in.

He had been there earlier. He visited at their home. He had left too early, so Natalia's heart was sore. She felt she had missed something. It was so cozy being near him in spite of the social rules that made them stiff and distant with each other. Those social rules protected her from much. Later, she would know how much.

What was all this her mother was talking of? What did it mean? She knew there was no point in blaming her loving, fragile mother for speaking her mind. She tried to be mature. There was an emotional repression common to many Russian aristocrats that made them keep more personal, intense feelings mostly to themselves (unless they were of anger or disapproval) while the person showed a demeanor calm as a glassy sea on a still day. It did not help her here. Her mother's fear was contagious. The regal/painful emotional repression that allowed only rage, contempt, disapproval, and a certain drama of character to show through sometimes led to meltdowns. Natalia felt so unsure that she wished to find solace again in the religion she'd known of since childhood. To find peace, she'd turn to church doctrine.

Chapter 5
A Train in the Cold

Katerina needed to go home. Her large eyes, which often had a hypnotic effect on others, were mirthless. She was at the train station waiting for the train which was a bit late. She knew her husband would be on it. She was annoyed because the train was late. Many other things annoyed her – her worries over her fifteen-year-old son and her nine-year-old daughter, her grief that often lingered in the back of her mind over her baby that had died before being able to talk, the weather, her depressing preoccupation with rivers (such a mystery to her), her boredom and irritation with her marriage to a man she used to love, and the fact that she was leaving this city sooner than she wished.

Her husband was named Constantine. He was not very excited at the idea of seeing his very pretty wife again. He was usually polite to her verbally. He was even a little in love with her. He had been her first lover, of course. He had been hoping to find a woman like that so long ago, and he had succeeded. He knew his wife did not like his first name. This bothered him. He had wed her mainly to take her off the hands of a relative who did not wish to financially support her any longer. It was not a perfect way to begin a marriage. Another problem had been that his wife did not enjoy attending church as much as he did. They came to love their children. They both managed servants and money well. The wife was not the best mother but was emotionally very responsive to her offspring. Katerina had a personality like a delicate flower that opens and closes only under certain conditions. She was very tricky to get along with. His wife's growing coldness to him was not something Constantine let trouble himself much. He was too scared to ask her if she still loved him. He was not a very brave man but was stronger than his wife knew.

Sergei was at the train station as well. Unfortunately, he saw Katerina. He saw right then he could ruin both of their lives if he did what he was considering doing. It was just a whim. He knew he probably wouldn't do it. He was so shallow; even real love was not something he was sure to be loyal to. He was attracted to her almost immediately and almost completely forgot about Natalia. Attraction can be a blessing of Heaven or a poisonous vine. A sinner is sometimes too confused to tell the difference. He could forget things very quickly. He was so spoiled; he did not have qualms about the consequences of what he was thinking of – to get this woman pregnant regardless of her legal husband and to see if he could flaunt this in public. Then, he might forget her. He developed feelings for women very fast, so here he had felt a crush on this woman very quickly, like someone who has eaten too much but wants stolen candy. He did not see how his hopes for this future relationship would demote him so much in the eyes of society, even in the perceptions of those who claimed to approve of it or envy it. His high standing meant much to him. He was much too competitive against other men.

Katerina saw him looking at her and was disgusted. She understood loss better than he did.

Her husband got off the train to speak with her. He had many times done some correct husbandly things like hand her into carriages and refuse to be too rough in manners with her no matter how long their arguments lasted.

Constantine noticed the stubborn-looking Sergei staring at his elegant wife, the chilled and uneasy Katerina, and the faithful husband was offended but kept his attention mostly on his wife's eyes. He was there to escort her home by train because he wanted to be with her even though she enjoyed traveling alone almost as much as traveling with someone. He started a conversation with her about their children. He knew this would be agreeable to her.

Sergei did a very rude thing. He kept looking, with his face blank, at the wife.

Chapter 6
Broken Love and Pretty Dances

What happened again and again in the social circles that Natalia lived in was a worn out, heartbreaking situation caused by the fact that these people had enough money (were rich) and free time to mess up their lives very much, so they did just that. Natalia decided not to be a part of this pattern that caused so much loss and pain. Therefore, she made one of the most upsetting, smart, and dramatic decisions of her life; she decided she would not wed Sergei. She suspected in her innocent and somewhat naive (and consequently much smarter than many of the worldly people around her with more experience and sins) heart that the gorgeous man she had dreamed of being married to was like someone who enjoyed taking walks in other people's gardens without permission. She could see now that it was as if he liked to smell all the pretty flowers but did not wish to pay the cost of buying them. There was something sneaky about his eyes. It was as though he would like to gossip about people behind their backs. She wondered what his secrets were but was too afraid to ask. What if it destroyed her to learn the answers? After so much soul-searching and many prayers, she ended up in tears or fell asleep mumbling. She began to see it would hurt even more to marry this man than it would to let him go. She was devastated. He did not inspire in her the feelings of safety, beauty, and sentiment that religion did. She decided she would tell him soon. She decided she would be dressed in black and then tell him at the ball. This was a serious decision, so it needed a serious occasion.

Before going, she sat at home. She was so very still. Slowly, silently, and one by one, the tears began to fall. She was, as yet, unready for the ball.

Dressed in a lovely black gown with fancy details, she walked into the event feeling almost like she was going to her own execution. Her mother and several friends were with her. Her mother tried to be stoic, but occasionally her eyes glistened. She knew why her daughter was at this dance. Natalia had worn gloves not just because she loved gloves and fancy accessories but also so she would not have to touch the man she was about to be brokenhearted over. She, who was always so composed when in public and on display, was so nervous she was scared she would stumble in her high heels. She felt like a little girl. Her face was stiff, except that her lips trembled. She began to smile at people. It made her feel more secure.

After several dance partners and a meaningful glance at her mother, the cherished daughter was at last in the arms of the man she still had such romantic feelings for. Iron willpower began to control her lips. She opened her mouth to speak, but it stayed still because she was so nervous. Her eyes were wide. Her heart was beating so hard; she wondered if it would hurt if it went any faster.

The cold, distant look on his face that had often spooked her before was in place. He spoke first.

"What opens a pretty mouth but stays inside?" She found the courage to answer.

"Harsh words," she replied.

His whole expression changed. For the first time, she saw more of the real man behind the charm. He looked so angry. No female had ever spoken to him quite like this. His thoughts scrambled, so he struggled to come up with a witty yet evasive line to say.

She swallowed hard. She tried to figure out what it was in his eyes she was so afraid of. She spoke again with difficulty.

"I believe with all my heart I cannot marry you. So, there is no need for you to continue your attentions. I fear your heart lies elsewhere. Perhaps it loves some girl more than me, or maybe you love yourself more than me."

To her shock and horror, he did not give her time to continue. He stopped dancing. He walked away. Others noticed. She stood still as a stone for a very few moments. But a savior showed up. A young man she hardly knew walked up to her and asked her to dance. His face showed polite coolness and a little pity for what she had just endured from her former dance partner. She smiled and gratefully accepted. People stopped looking at her so much. This helped her regain more of her poise.

Chapter 7
Love Spell

Katerina resisted Sergei for a long time. She did a good job. She knew he was handsome and attractive. But she was not attracted to him. His sensual nature irritated her depressed mind. She had a strong will behind a fluttering heart. She saw him again and again on the street, at the theater, out of the corner of her eyes while she talked to her husband, and so on. There were breaks to this nonsense. He could not simply quit his life to follow her around. But he'd become a little neglectful of his duties. She felt sorry for herself. Her husband seldom noticed what this predator of a man was doing, but when Constantine did notice it, he merely seemed annoyed in front of his lovely wife. He hid his deeper feelings of hatred for Sergei. He did not realize how much he hurt his wife's feelings and pride by not seeming more jealous as a man. Slowly, reluctant Katerina's soul began to respond to the attentions of the other man. She tried to hide it and respond with wit to keep him at a distance.

"Why do you take the trouble to pursue another man's wife? Isn't it more trouble than it's worth?"

He replied, "It's worth whatever you say it is."

He was not giving up. He was pretending to be more concerned with her feelings and future than he really was. Since his failure with Natalia, he had polished some of his tactics for dealing with women. His remark sparked a passionate outburst of feeling from his prey. She spoke in loud tones of the dangers of temptation and how she would hate to lose her beloved, elevated place in society. Then, she walked away rapidly and in a rage. She tried to hide the fact that she felt a little helpless. Her husband witnessed this conversation from a distance and decided very firmly to speak to his wife in private. When she was not expecting it or was ready for it, he opened the conversation.

"How are you? You were upset with a young man recently. What are your relations with him? They should not have been kept from me."

There was a long silence. Many thoughts went quickly through the wife's troubled mind. She struggled to form a coherent reply. She did not wish to tell her husband everything, not because of her attraction for another but because she was angry with her mate. She wanted to keep a great deal locked in her heart. It had been so long since her husband had lavished much attention on her. In public, it was often clear that he did not take her very seriously. It embarrassed her, but she kept silent about it.

Slowly, through stiff lips, she pronounced the words, "There is nothing you need to know."

He knew his wife was suffering. He felt a little guilty. He changed his expression to one of husbandly affection. He said, "I refuse to offend you or me with questions I have no reason to ask."

She wished he would say more but felt there was no point in telling him if he could not see that himself. She decided to be a bit selfish. She looked at him with all the charm she could muster.

She said in a silky tone, "You know I am your wife. No other man gets wifely devotion from me or ever has." It was true.

But unfortunately, later it was not.

It took the heartless tempter, who wanted what was not his and who was thrilled all the more because it belonged to another man, nine months from the beginning of his insulting nagging to debase, fool, and attract this high-class (if occasionally flighty) woman into the type of sin he fancied most at this point in his life. She was incredibly angry with him, herself, the people who knew and who judged (rightly), and the people who might find out. She felt sickened. She had wanted change, security, love, and excitement. But she felt so disillusioned; she suffered from a confusing mental paralysis. He wondered if she was pregnant by him. She was not. She screamed at him because of the risks they were taking. She wanted to cry. She wanted to go home. She wanted to go back to her husband. She did not know if she should tell Constantine or not. What would he do or say? The questions put sheer terror in her heart. Even she did not understand all the reasons why she wanted to go back to her sarcastic, yet solid, husband instead of staying with her new lover – the man with a masterful soft touch but hard eyes. She loved this new man, but her mind was shattered. She was disgusted by her illicit lover's big ego. After an affair so short, her deluded mind was forgetting some of the details so soon that it was shameful.

She went home. She tried to act as normally as she could. But her brief fling with wild behavior had turned her into a shadow.

Her husband wondered what had caused the change in her behavior. He was determined to find the answer. His mind went back to when she had been a new bride. Whatever tenderness he was capable of brought a slight smile to his lips as he fondly recalled her at her wedding. He disciplined himself to remember so many things about that event and a few weeks before and after it. He remembered the tilt of her head, her big smile, and wide eyes, and he began to remember other details about that blessed yet flawed time, the weather, other people's voices, and the white and holy dress that the shy bride wore.

Finally, after days of worry for both of them, screaming arguments because of her evasiveness, hours of silent agony coupled with confusion for the husband, and long stares at her face by him, he took her by the shoulders and did not let go until she had confessed. She did not go into many details. She felt better and worse. She was nauseated and exhausted. She felt better because the truth had been told, but she felt worse because she felt so mired in sin that her depression turned her face to stone. Her sadness drained her until it was difficult to even make basic decisions she had made before with ease in her daily life. She was a soft flower that had begun to wilt. The poison of an illicit lover was very powerful and worked very fast. She became confused easily and did not know much about how to continue life with her family. Emotional pains that were tolerable before were now so crushing that she had no ideas for coping with them.

When her mate learned of her infidelity, he hid his pain well. He was a government man, and so he had hidden feelings for years so as not to seem a fool. His feelings were hurt, for he loved his wife. He was very shocked she had taken another man. He knew the foolish affair was over because she had sworn in tears that it was. She did not have the energy to lie. The husband showed his utter disapproval to his wife.

Chapter 8
Lovesick

Natalia had a big, Russian nervous breakdown. She bitterly joked that she enjoyed it. But she usually had no sense of humor at this point in her life. She tried her best to forget some things that made her miserable about the man she'd left behind. She shoved to the back of her heart and mind little details about the way he moved, some words he'd said, and other memories that had made such a strong impression on her before. This disaster made her the center of attention quite often, which she liked. She did not always choose to show how much she enjoyed it.

There was no way to control the gossip that this big romantic disaster had caused. Visitors came and went. Some were young. Some were old. They were all curious. Some expressed true sympathy. Others said the proper things while a slight sneer showed on their faces. Her mother tried desperately to control the ugly situation out of sympathy for her daughter and maternal, deeply rooted fears about what other people would think. Her father wore a stern expression on his face quite often these days. He did not show his feelings much, but he was brokenhearted for his daughter. She was in a pitiful state. However, the satisfaction in knowing she had made a good decision (even though it had caused misery, shock, and regret) put an ethereal smile on her face a few times, as did the thought that SHE had left HIM, and people knew it. A virginal instinct told her he had not had the satisfaction he craved because he had not been the one to tell her she must go. She had heard he loved another woman. He did not even try to hide it because his taste in manners was so poor. This next female prey was not even free, but wed. Natalia felt this showed just how far his status had sunk. She wondered if the man she'd once cared for so much was even fully aware of his sinking position. Was he so arrogant that he believed he could get away with anything? Natalia knew it did not work this way in their high society, not even for a man like him. Also, it did not work that way in the military. She still felt stupid, but the feeling of loss was slowly going away. It was like the dew evaporating in the morning. Love faded and wilted in her heart poisoned by lies. Her body trembled for hours every day. She saw light bruises on her body, and she had no memory of how they'd gotten there. They must've been caused by her own clumsiness. She hated how awkward she often was these days. It embarrassed her in front of company. She was no more happy with people she had close relationships with. She was lonely half the time. She turned to God. This was very personal for her, and she did not share it often with others. Lessons of Christianity showed the correct way to heal without hurting others.

Some of these lessons surprised her.

She overheard quotes as people came and went:

"She should not have turned him down."

"He did not even propose. Stop listening to the worst gossips. She told him she did not wish the courtship to continue."

"I do not understand why she was so picky. He was such a nice, charming man!"

"If you trust someone who told you he was nice, you are one big glass of stupidity!"

"That man was a tiger on the hunt, with lovely manners on the outside but the heart of an alcoholic peasant." This was uttered by some random snob who, nevertheless, saw deeply into people's souls without difficulty.

"Which peasant?"

"Oh, shut up."

"You're missing the point."

"No, I'm not."

On and on it went.

It gave the girl, who had enjoyed such bright dreams for her wedding, headaches and nightmares to know he was already showing attraction to another woman. But it increased her faith in her ability to choose well. She saw painfully clearly that she had broken a relationship off with a man who was very fickle.

There was one visitor who was more solemn than all the others combined. He almost never saw her face-to-face. When he did, he never said a word of reproach or cruelty. He never once whined about the fact that she had shown no interest in marrying him. He looked at her very hard if he looked directly at her. This made her think. He usually spoke with her family or visitors instead of her. She was tired. He knew she did not see how weak she was. Most of what burned his soul he hid behind a polite face. The mother did not tell him much about her stricken daughter. Her crafty, maternal mind was testing him.

Chapter 9
Resolve

Katerina was scared. Some fears she understood, but many others were a mystery to her. She spent hours trying to think what it was she was afraid of.

She was so tired from her doomed attempt at a sordid romantic life with a man besides her legal husband that it was very difficult for Sergei to try to woo her again. It was very hard to even see her. She noticed him rarely. She had begun to simply act, as often as she could, as if the whole mess of infidelity had not happened. This made no sense. It put a fog in her head. On her worst days, she made bad decisions all day.

There were whispers. Her past lover, a man she now wished she'd never loved, had not been completely quiet about their little, shameful affair. She felt completely betrayed. Love had not solved her problems. But love was ruling her life. She did not see that. She might have found a way out of her troubles if she had known that.

Her husband still loved her a little but refused to let her or anyone else know it. Their offspring knew there was a problem but did not know what it was. So, the son and the daughter lived in confusion. They suffered from bouts of sadness like black clouds. Sometimes, they began to talk to their parents only to go silent in the middle of a sentence.

When her pathetic, tempting love affair with Sergei started again, she was so shocked at herself that she wept every day. She did not fully know herself anymore. This was very painful to her. Her personality seemed to have split in half – one part was her, and the other part was controlled by her heartless lover. He charmed her. He toyed with her emotions. He distracted her and lied to her. Sometimes he lied just to lie or because it was easier to lie. He was in love but felt no remorse. He had a softness of heart that replaced her husband's coolness. One of Sergei's lies was to say he was never attracted to other ladies. These ladies never warmed to him. In the back of his mind, he thought of others if Katerina was not with him. He thought of them more and more and then with greater longing as he grew a little bored with his current lady. Legal marriage was not possible for their union in Russia because the laws were that only the wronged party (the faithful husband of Katerina) could obtain the divorce, and she would not be allowed to remarry or keep her children. Sergei did not care that the loss of her children (she still felt them in her heart like they were babies, even though they were older) would grieve her. He pretended to care.

The flower that was Katerina had continued to die and lose its pretty scent. The husband, of course, found out quickly that this depraved woman was back with the same man she'd sinned with before. Constantine's anger knew no bounds. He had been a little more tolerant with her before when she had strayed from their marriage, even though he disapproved, because he still loved her. He had punished her while trying to keep this love a secret. He wondered if she knew no matter how clever he was. But this second time, he became completely bitter to her. His love died in an instant. He was angry at what she was doing to him, his career, and his children. He felt she was a total fool for taking such risks. Did she think he was too stupid to get a divorce?

The unfaithful wife's resolve to resist another man and keep a certain amount of honor had turned into a resolve to stay with her new love.

Chapter 10
Katerina and the Water

She was obsessed with water before she loved Sergei. But now that strange love for the sacred, clear liquid had taken a darker turn. She loved to stand by the river. Watching the flow calmed her down and helped her to sort her thoughts. The pretty water reminded her of fairytales, sacred rituals, and purity of spirit. She even went into a dreamy mild trance while looking at water if she stared long enough. It kept alive the child in her. But now that child was dying, her unholy love for a man she knew too little was showing her too much. The pleasure she used to feel looking at water, even if it was just in a beautiful glass, was now beginning to be tainted. She hated this but obeyed temptation. The water that had even helped to ease the grief over her dead child was losing its hold on her mind as Sergei took more control over her. When she looked at water now, it did not comfort her as much as it used to. On rare occasions, it even made her think of the idea of drowning. She was not suicidal. It was just a vague idea that oppressed her. So many times in the past she had visited bodies of water, and she had not felt lonely even if alone. It had sometimes irked her to have her husband with her by the river. Since her affair with Sergei had begun again, she felt shame when the light reflected off the water. She knew she was madly risking her place in high society by cheating on her spouse. Her classy position and lifestyle had meant much to her, so she hated the fear of its loss even for love. She hated the man she was in love with, and she hated her husband while missing him.

Chapter 11
Vladimir at Home

Vladimir enjoyed his lifestyle. He liked being outside. The mist gave him peace. The fields made him feel secure. He loved farming. He had wanted to share it with his beloved lady, but she was elusive. He also feared she did not have many ideas in her head about farming, and she probably would not care for it much. But he held the lovely notion in his mind, all the same, of his future wife (if he could ever get her to agree) walking across his land, appreciating the efforts mankind can make on nature to produce crops and sustain life. He knew many people in his social circle did not care about farming at all. He did not care that they did not care. He often did not care much about the rich people he knew who would have detested to farm. Their minds seemed dull to him as if they had drowned years ago.

At home, half the time he was happy, and half the time he was sad. He had known loneliness. He often got along with the people who were not in his class. This was good because many of them were needed to work on his estate. However, he did not form deep friendships with them. He was a strange, solitary man who rarely dreamed at night. For years, his dreams had bored him. He woke up from them in a bad mood. He was, of course, often very busy. His positive feelings for farming had given him a positive view of life. His struggles with depression never lasted longer than a few weeks.

He still loved only one woman, so he could not seem to give up the hope of being with her. His head tried to tell his heart it was unrealistic, but his heart kept telling his head to be quiet. He was muddled in the mind on the subject of religion. He knew he must be clear on it to please the woman he refused to stop being in love with. He wondered if God acted more often like a judge or a father. He couldn't remember exact scriptures very well. He doubted. He knew he must clear this up like a bad storm. If he doubted too much, his wife (if he could obtain this desire) would feel he accused not just God and angels but also her. She would not tolerate this. She was so sure about ideas mysterious to him that his love led to faith as he learned. He read and read more. He laughed at himself.

For years, he had done a good job at his work. But relating to people very different from him confused him, so he tended to keep changing the subject while talking to them. He liked himself almost as much as the bride he hoped for. He thought he had done her a great service by not saying to her or others the many words that were in his mind about her badly chosen love for another and her public foolishness. He was showing his credit for her intelligence with silence by using this lack of words to tell her he assumed she knew he was upset but still enamored of her. His sorrow at her plight as well as her downcast eyes in his presence had made his love even stronger than his fear.

At the home he had tailored to fit his personality, he contemplated religion, why badly behaving plants can drive even someone who loves them crazy, vodka, Natalia, Russia, and the fact that one of Russia's biggest problems was that all those in high society knew one another at least a bit, which led to some of them not liking one another a lot. He was still not completely sure of what to do or when to do it. He thought of all this over his cup of tea.

Chapter 12
A New Child

The wronged husband of this story had a distant friend named Galina Voloskaya. She was a countess and very proud of it. She almost never looked anyone in lower society in the eye. Ironically, she was not extremely cruel. Some of her class did not care that her country needed some changes or if a peasant died of alcoholism or poverty. And, in truth, some of the changes suggested for Russia's woes were stupid or simply immoral. Some of the nobility were not that worried because there were so many peasants; if a lot died, there would still be enough to make Russia. Galina often hid any kindness she might or might not feel behind a polite expression of genius on her placid face. This made her eyes glow in a mysterious way. When Constantine's wife became unfaithful, Galina knew it very soon afterwards. She behaved wisely in who she told and did not tell. She tried to see if she could get the straying cat of a wife to underestimate her. When the countess learned Katerina knew she was pregnant, the countess made sure to convey the news to Constantine as well as the information on who the real father was. Galina had calculated correctly that Katerina would not tell her husband of the baby but would tell her lover.

Katerina had been at home. She had gotten her unofficial husband to come to her so she could try to speak to him with no other soul around. This was hard considering her loss of status among the servants who suspected the problem. But Sergei had shown up. He looked wonderful. His eyes glittered like a hard jewel, which should have warned her but did not. She was very worried. "I have something important to tell you." His shallow mind was a little shocked.

"I am pregnant." She lowered her eyelids. She looked so sad.

He was, not fully understanding the situation, overjoyed. He had longed for this cursed love's blessing as he saw it.

She began to see he assumed wrongly. She became angry. She was a mother and could see his reaction was to be elated yet immature. She still loved him, so it hurt her to see him disappoint her so. She also saw the beast thought that it was his. Why were so many men so egotistical?

"It's my husband's."

His good mood shattered. He looked confused. There was a long pause. He stared at her.

"Are you sure?"

"Yes," she answered. She was sure of the timing. She had known no confusion over it. Her contempt for his reaction increased.

It was never clear to many people how a servant's friend had told another servant, who had told a princess, who had told Galina about the baby and its paternity. It was also unclear how expensive this was, but this process had worked.

When Katerina learned her husband knew her two secrets (a baby and which man it went with), she cried for two days. She became paranoid. She told her lover what her husband by law knew, and her lover was humiliated. He began to lose more of his love for her. He did not tell her this. He helped care for her. Galina and Constantine became closer friends.

The wife told no other of her condition. She simply let it show when it became obvious because she was not hiding herself in the country or another nation. The man who had been thwarted in his hopes of fatherhood was not very happy she showed herself in this way. Illogically, this badly matched couple had alternately flaunted and then hidden their affair again and again. So, some were not sure what to gossip about.

The real father felt a love for this unborn child, which he forced himself to feel in spite of the mother. He also felt it a victory over her lover. He was pleased Sergei was not happy about not being a father. What right did this selfish man have to think of bringing a bastard child into the world? It was such a cruel thing to do to a baby. Constantine saw better than Sergei how unsuited the second man was to fatherhood.

Chapter 13
Running Out of Time

Sergei was destined to lose the race. He did not handle females perfectly, human or otherwise. So, since the horse he would be racing on was a mare, he was in trouble. It would be a dangerous race. Some of the other riders destined to lose this race were a little crazy in the head. There would be obstacles for the horse to jump, so if a horse decided not to obey (which was a probability), things could go very wrong very quickly. But who cared? At least one person who didn't care was Sergei Shermetov. He liked danger and cared less and lesser as the days went by about the potential consequences of his actions. He had been angry and shocked to find out that a few military people he knew were avoiding him or had lost a bit of respect for him after his fall from grace in his personal life. Upon hearing of his loss of the princess and liaison with a married woman of lower status, they had lost a bit of faith in him as a military man. They would have lost a lot more faith if they'd been smarter.

One person who was very worried was Anastova. She was worried for her lover's safety (but not much because she was offended that he had shown so little concern for that worry). Mostly, she feared the devastating emotional effects that attending this race with her husband would bring. It was twice as scary because the tsar would be there. He could look through people like they were not there if he wanted to.

The tsar was already a bit bored in the crowd. Half his mind was a mess, so he hoped this little distraction of a horse race would clear it up. He looked around a lot. He did notice, for just brief moments, Anastova fidgeting with her binoculars and biting her lip. The tsar thought she seemed a bit silly and prone to fretting over ridiculous problems that she didn't see that she didn't need to entangle herself in. He knew about Sergei, too, and felt he had the sensitivity to others of a chunk of dirt. The tsar was not very interested in these two people. He turned his attention to the court and the racetrack.

Constantine Anastov glared at his wife. He'd been trying to decide whether or not to begin a divorce. In the past, he and his wife had disagreed on how many children to have. Was this why she strayed? His pride felt battered. He wondered how a divorce over something so sordid would affect his career. But it was more sordid to stay with a woman who had a side dish. This was how he had come to think of the man who had stolen his wife. Why was his wife such an overly emotional, sinful fool? She was an embarrassment. How had the shy, uncertain girl he had once carefully held in his arms turned into this hard, distant person who sat right next to him but did not look at him? Her face was rigid. Why was she so devoted to Sergei when she was so annoyed with the same man? Constantine's hatred lit up his soul and set-in motion his thoughts. He found it disgusting that she now belonged to another man but still wanted to hang on to her legal position as his wife in a pathetic attempt to retain her position in society. Who did she think she was fooling? He knew Russia had problems and some of the suggestions to fix it or change it were of the worst sort, and all his stupid wife could do was have an illicit affair. She continued to try to get money from Constantine, too. This made him so angry; it was as if his mind was on fire. He knew her rich lover spent lavishly on her. It hurt Constantine that another man now brought her romantic gifts. He barely noticed that the race had begun. He didn't care if Sergei broke his neck. Constantine was determined to keep his child, once born, away from this man. It irritated and scared the father that during the pregnancy, he had not been able to keep the growing child away from Sergei. Anastov found it difficult to keep his state of mind about his wife from affecting his work. Now, when people petitioned him with their requests, he was so angry that it was hard to focus; he tended to pause in every few phrases when answering.

Even though he still loved her, Sergei had not tried to help Anastova much with the fears she had about his part in this race. She had a certain magical effect on him that no one else ever had, but he (more often than not) did what he wanted whether she worried over it or not. He did not soothe her fears the way her husband once had. Sergei pretended to love more than he really did.

The regrets were growing in the woman. Her son and daughter knew she had cheated on their father. They were not in a forgiving mood about her. They did not understand very well why she had done it. They were afraid of the evil in her character. They did not love her anymore. She could not see many situations clearly anymore. Sadness mixed up her thoughts. Desire can be a powerful force for healing; it's so much so that even the wish to get well can bring a certain amount of cure. But out of control and out of bounds of propriety desire can do more damage than a faithless debtor realizes to be happening.

It was beautiful to see the powerful horses move. The cooperation between horses and masters resulted in the animals running over the ground in a motion akin to a boat successfully sailing over rough water. Half of them were smarter than their riders. The animals were fast yet careful. Three decided not to obey their riders for a few seconds at a time. They slowed down out of fear or pranced nervously. When their frantic riders could get them to continue, they were straining to catch up to the others. There was not a lot of trust between animals and riders in this race. It was an almost comical flaw. Before it was over, two magnificent animals had fallen. Both of their masters were in pain. One had a cracked bone. Sergei's overbearing attitude had shown in the way he rode; it had upset his horse and thrown off the rhythm between the horse and the rider. The winner of the race felt a little let down because, though unhurt, he had been competing against people he felt were bigger fools than four-footed animals any day of the week. He was a snob, but he was a snob with no broken bones.

The tsar felt a slight urge to laugh, but there was no way he would admit it.

Constantine did not care who had won the race. Oddly, he felt sympathy for the animals. He did not know why this change had come over him. He had never felt very sorry for an animal before. The prospect of a divorce from his wife tormented him due to the heavy emotional loads it would place on the rest of their family. But his trust in his wife had become a dead vine.

After the race, Constantine and his wife had an argument so hot and bitter that he could not bring himself to look at her for hours afterward. He decided to begin a divorce.

Chapter 14
Losing at the Game of Love

Maria's mate had failed again at another one of his fool's errands. The meaning of that sentence is that he had once again failed to cheat on his wife with one of the many girls he had targeted. His wife knew. She knew about most of this sort of stupidity of her husband. Her fury and hurt were so great that she behaved like a stabbed lioness. Her tears and tantrums were frequent, of course, and one of her favorite things to do was scream at her husband until she cried.

Her husband did something very shocking. He slowly began to see reason. He began to see the effects of how cruel he had been. He began to see the horrible effect this was having on his children. The children did not know the details, of course, because their mother protected them from that. They did not see the list the wife had penned of female names of people who had turned her husband down. They were servants, other men's wives, ballet dancers, and singers, and it did not end there. Sometimes, in her hysteria, she had such contempt for him because not only did he try to be unfaithful, he could not even do it. A brave ballet dancer had even given him a hard slap when their conversation had taken a turn so ugly that she realized he wanted her to be his for a few hours instead of his real wife. He was a coward and had done nothing about it in spite of his high rank. This was very lucky for the dancer because treating a man of his position like that might have gotten her severe persecution. His wife knew of the slap and thought it was funny. It salved her hurt feelings a little.

His bad lifestyle took its toll; he became ill. He was very sick and had a lot of time to think and feel. He began to see he would lose everything if he succeeded at his sinful endeavors. He began to see what Anastova's lover could not see – that some pleasures were a path to destruction that his rank would not save a man from. Anastova's name was close to a name that meant to come back from the dead, but she was not living up to it. These and other morbid thoughts went through his mind as he suffered in his body and his conscience taught his mind. His wife had loudly threatened divorce more than three times. He did not know why he had thought he might get away with straying from a woman so prone to anger. He saw that what some men call a philosophy of excuses was claiming the right to be selfish and stupid. He saw this was like a road that did not lead to any place.

Sometimes, the life he had which demanded so much attention, etiquette, detail in dress, and energy would still leave him depleted, but he decided he would no longer respond by following women who did not want him. He had never hated his wife much. He had even loved her.

When the doctor told him that he would not die of his illness, he was overjoyed.

But to go to a very different subject, Anastova had a terrible argument with her husband when she found out he would divorce her. She would not make a firm resolve to be faithful but was not ready for a divorce. Her husband was unmoved by her rages and tears. He did not pity her. He saw more than she did of what this was doing to his son and daughter. He hated their mother for not knowing it. Security was worth much to Constantine. He did not see how he could be secure with a wife like this. He saw her as inhuman. She did not know Constantine had overcome his fear and passive nature long enough to shove her lover in front of witnesses.

Constantine's heart was a little cracked, and he could not bring himself to live still with the one who had tried to completely break it. He told his wife to live elsewhere. He resented it that she had his name.

Chapter 15
A True Friend Intervenes

Galina knew better than to try to be a mother to Constantine's offspring. The wounds were still too new to the son's and daughter's feelings. She decided to be more like an aunt to them. She took them to church when their father permitted it. So, she was one of the people in the back of the son's mind on a really bad day that he had that included a train ride.

The son had ridden on a train with an older relative he did not know well. He did not hate them, but he did not love them much. This older person had chattered on and on about nothing, or so it seemed to the teenager. The younger one was an intense individual who had not tried romantic love. He hated his mother's rich lover with a passion.

When they got off the train at the busy station and were waiting to catch another train, Anastova's boy walked until there was a little distance between him and his relative. He walked slowly, and his mind was deep in thought. After a little while, every thought was bad. He was scared for his sister. He felt little hope for his new sibling still growing. He was so scared the baby would be harmed or would lead an unhappy life. Sadness and confusion took control of him.

He was so tense. He thought of every one of his family members. He felt his mother had chosen her morally filthy lover over her son. He began looking hard at the trains. They were not going extremely fast, but the noise was still annoying. Love (not romance) and hate mingled in the boy. This was very dangerous. It became hard to think. He was embarrassed by his mother. Death seemed like peace. It also seemed like a way to shame his mother even more. Many people would find out about it if he decided to kill himself by being hit by a train. He was so disgusted that he could hardly stand it. He was so afraid of the pain. Oddly, he felt like maybe he would be a coward if he didn't do it. He tried to fight off the temptation to get rid of himself, but he was smiling slightly at the idea.

A cold rain began to fall. It began to clean the dirty train station a little.

The sad teenager looked to his side and saw a disheveled peasant man several feet away. The peasant was dangerously close to the rails. Constantine's poor son did not know if this man was extremely drunk. He decided he was probably not looking at a drunken man but a very tired one. He could tell the peasant was aware of the danger but did not care. Their troubles were very different, but the poor man had been considering the same type of death that the wealthier man's teenager had just almost decided upon. The peasant was much closer to liking the idea of an early grave. He laughed a little. Then, he abruptly stopped. When the peasant took a little step closer to the rails, the fearful son of Constantine, friend of Galina, Christian Russian, and the son of a splitting couple (for all these were one lonely boy) yelled to him to back up. He knew this peasant was deliberately risking his life. When the peasant did not obey, the boy ran to him and grabbed him by the arm, so he could not rush forward. He was stronger than the peasant, so this was easy. The hot anger was still in him, but his mind began to frost over with relief at saving this poor man.

More people noticed them and began to stare and talk. More began to realize a tragedy had just been averted.

When Constantine found out from Galina about this episode, his hatred for his wife grew. He did not know why his son had chosen to tell Galina. Katerina still loved her son, but it was a selfish love.

The father decided to take his son and daughter to church more often.

Chapter 16
Second Chance

It is very hard to let a dream die, and some dreams will not die at all. Love works with faith to keep them alive.

Vladimir's love remained in pain and the absence of the beloved. Why did his heart work backwards? But he held true to the faith that perhaps Natalia would still be his wife. He also needed to continue to sort another kind of faith out in his mind. She would be insulted if someone suggested to her a husband who did not believe in God. The Father, Jesus, and the Holy Ghost were very real to her. That was the light she ran to when life was full of shadows or confusion. He believed in God because she did. His faith was very simple. It was his mind that was complicated and fearful. He had problems with various types of faith. Logic got in the way of the child like beauty that he needed. He knew this but didn't know what to do to cure it. He thought maybe marriage would cure it. He understood the basic ideas, but many details of Christian faith escaped him. Many in his country were superstitious. This did not confuse him much. He finally decided if the Trinity was real, then Natalia was a little like one of His angels. He did not know if this was very theologically in a strict sense sound but was comforted by the thought.

His home made him calm. He hoped it would calm her, too. He knew he would have to pay attention to this love the way he did a seedling. Some seedlings were so delicate; if handled much, they died.

The man who had never shamed her or made her feel stupid for her mistakes began to seem more and more appealing to Natalia. He corrected his style in his marriage proposal. She talked about herself for a little while, talked about church for a little while, and then accepted. It was unusual to give a speech like this at a proposal, but he did not mind.

She thought it was funny that her religious faith was so solid, while he had so many questions about God. Spiritual questions that seemed very complicated to him had simple answers to her.

When Natalia moved to her new husband's home, it was a big change and shock for her. It was a big adjustment to her to be away from her parents. She was still glad she had rejected Sergei. Her choice of Vladimir felt more secure to her. Even she could not understand all of what it was about Sergei that scared her so. It was inevitable that she would see him once in a while due to their positions in society. She did not still love him, but her heart still hurt because of their shared memories. She knew of his theft of another man's wife that he had taken in a sordid love. She knew he did not care what regrets he gave to Katerina. She also knew he would come to have regrets himself. She wondered if he hated it that he had lost her and that she had wed Vladimir.

He did.

Natalia liked the fields. She had not known she would like them so much. They gave her some peace after her turmoil. She had to learn what her new life would be like. She was shy and hesitant about learning to get along with her husband's staff, but she believed she could learn to relate to different people. She hoped he would help her.

The newly married couple tended to talk of religion over long meals and hot drinks until the wife laughed about her husband's doubts and told him to be quiet.

Chapter 17
Real Father

Two lovers who had rejected some of society's rules and Constantine's wishes had not known they would be so rejected by society. A bad mother always deserves punishment. Walking around pregnant with one man's child while she met another man to act like his wife was so unattractive to many in Russian society. They barely understood her motives. There were those who did not care if it was a sin, or there were those that envied them, but this did not make their position easy. Nevertheless, the two locked in this strange love continued to run away from Eden. Justice's destiny was to be measured out.

Constantine had tried to stay near his unborn child, but Anastova had strayed much. There came a time when Constantine was stunned to get a telegram from Sergei saying Anastova's child was about to be born. Constantine knew the time was realistic, but what shocked him was who the telegram was from. He hurried to be near his wife. Sergei was there and others who were medically necessary. Constantine refused to go in to see her, but he could hear enough from her and the talk of others to know she was not doing well. This did not shock him because he knew her recent lifestyle had been such a strain on her. He told Sergei he had to leave, as this was not his child, and he had no right to be present. Sergei, his face stoic, left. The telegram had not softened his attitude towards his wife's paramour. Constantine had been bitter, as the pregnant woman had not lived with him until the child had been born, even though the parents could not relate to each other well enough to be in the same room. When he knew his new son had been born and was healthy, he burst into tears of relief and broke out in a cold sweat. He tried to keep a bit of dignified reserve even now in front of others. He could not hide his happiness upon hearing that his wife was doing so poorly that she had fainted. He would not have to talk with her. He made arrangements against her wishes that the baby would be home with him as soon as the child was ready. He looked forward to telling happy family news to his other son and daughter. He would be able to put some of their worries to rest. They did not know what to worry about and what not to. He did not care to learn the rest of the details of his wife's health.

Days later, he visited Katerina again. As she sat, her face was a mask of fury because he had taken the baby. She expected him to tell her how the child was doing — she did not even know its gender for sure. She had many questions. But though he knew she wanted to hear of her baby, he merely told her she was a divorced woman. She was so shocked that it took her a few moments to even cry. He had managed to get the divorce relatively quickly due to his high position. In her confused mind, she had even thought that maybe she would never be divorced. She had thought that for the sake of his job, he might refrain from such a drastic step. When she found the words, she loudly began questioning him about several things: how he had gotten the divorce so quickly, the baby, and his cold face.

Her beauty irritated him, as it belonged to someone else. He wondered why her degenerate lover was not with her. He silently turned and left.

Katerina was in deep shock and felt such loss. Her feelings were a little numb. She thought she and her lover might need to leave the country to try to find peace. She was so scared. Her love for Sergei was a little less attractive, since it was something she felt stuck with now that she was divorced. She wished she understood better what her fears were. Sergei was her strength, but she was scared he was attracted to other women. He denied it if she asked him of it, but he lied. He was still loyal to her, so she often believed him. Love did not matter as much to him as it did to her. He was ice and fire, which drew her to him, but she did not know that if she did not belong to someone else, he would not love her as much. He had never wanted to wed her as much as he had wanted to wed Natalia; even that desire had not been strong enough to coax the proper words out of his lips. His lips were better suited to lies.

She waited a few days. Then, she sent a servant with a note for her former husband. In it, she asked to see her baby and claimed motherly responsibility for all her offspring. What she got back was one of his servants handing her a note from Constantine and a letter from her son. All Constantine's note said was:

Read the message from your son.
Constantine

Her son's letter said:

I will be as blunt as you. Your daughter did not wish to write, as she is afraid of you, so I wrote for myself and for my sister. We are clearly not of as much interest to you as someone else is. You are not like the mother I once knew.

You have earned contempt. Do not visit.

Chapter 18
Crop of Sin

Forbidden fruit is destroyed when not in the hands of its proper owner. A farmer who has put so much work and love into planting will tend a plot of land until his work is over, but a thief will just steal the fruit and run. Katerina was beginning to comprehend just how hopeless her position was. Her timing was terrible. She regretted so many actions of hers. She could see Sergei did not have much sympathy and hated him for it. She began to doubt him more and more. He did not seem to have a solid plan for what they could do. Her mind began to unravel. She knew she was stared at with contempt even by girls much lower in society who had more virtue than her.

Sergei's career was a mess long ago. He hated this but pretended not to care. He hated that it was his own fault. The couple kept moving around. They had the money to keep making bad decisions. For thousands of years, many have approved of such behavior. Once in the country, a young teenaged girl who knew some of their story, even where she lived, laughed and jeered at Sergei right in front of Katerina and others. The teenager had walked right up to him and asked him if he knew a devil from an angel or a good girl from a radish. It was funny and very brave. The teenager's friends had laughed and others were surprised. The girl knew it was risky to talk to him that way but had not been able to help herself. It was fun, and she resented their high-class positions she did not have and would never have no matter how she behaved. Sergei silently let her talk to him like that.

Katerina knew she could never be fully happy with this new life of hers. Sergei had a nightmare in which he would never become a father. He did not think much about it, but variations of it became a recurring bad dream. When he shared this with Katerina, she told him she did not wish to be pregnant again so soon. He lost almost all his love for her, but she did not choose to notice. He knew he was letting Russia down. The country's turmoil could be used as a chance for sin to rule, and that would cause even more suffering. He began to hate the lack of energy and action in his life.

Sometimes, Katerina stared at a glass of water for a while before she drank it. She was trying to get that dreamy feeling of purity again, but it would not come.

She wanted to go home but did not know where her heart's home was. She missed her children but knew they did not want her. Somehow, Constantine was powerful enough. She knew he had been able to keep her from seeing her baby son. She had sent a nicely worded telegram to her oldest child but had gotten no reply.

Chapter 19
No More

These people did not talk much. They acted. Sometimes, they acted badly. Maybe, they should have talked more.

Katerina lied to Sergei by telling him it had never been a desire of hers to consider going back to her former husband. But she knew her first love would not take her back. She missed being a legal wife. Rarely, she became very excited by strange thoughts about how to get her old happiness back but then would patiently explain to herself that these made no sense. She was so sad that sometimes she sat still for hours. She was a wilted flower, and the decay was obvious.

The moral decline and its effects were no longer hidden by a beautiful, sincere gloss of classy manners. Her Russian sense of drama, when added to the cruelty in her life, had left her tired and argumentative.

Sergei still lied to Katerina by claiming he did not want to flirt with other women or go back to Natalia. Sometimes, she believed him. Sometimes, she strongly suspected he lied to her about this and other things. He was spooked by the fact that, once in a while, things she said made no sense. She did not seem to notice it. He was upset his job in the military was considered a joke, so he showed his anger too much. There was talk of war, but he knew he was not fully fit for it. He began to regret that he had sacrificed so much for her. She had been mysterious to him, but that lovely feeling was gone. She was a little too thin. She had not been underweight before meeting him. She had screaming fits, of course. Her eyes were so dull. When she slept poorly, she blamed him. The beloved's price had been too high. She still had her lover's comfort, but she felt that was the worst part. He began to see that she resented his love. His love no longer cleared her head. His handsome face upset her. This made her nervous.

He still had a gun due to the military. Whether or not he had a right to it by strict military standards, the fact remained that he had it. Once, they had an argument so terrible that she picked it up, knowing it was loaded, and threw it in a random fashion at him. Even she did not know all the reasons why she did this to a man she still loved. But that romantic, poetic fire was cooling little by little. Life seemed more and more meaningless. She saw too late that she had left a man who treated her a little like a queen for a man who treated her more and more like a servant. She had no ability now to forgive with a kind, true heart. That heart was heavy with sorrow and confusion. After she had thrown the gun, Sergei had picked it up off the floor where it had landed after bouncing off him. It had not gone off. He was so angry. With a tense, frozen look on his face, he unloaded it.

One day, he found a note written by her. It said nothing except that she had left the country.

Chapter 20
Aftermath of Loss

Companions (mostly males) of Sergei knew he had considered getting so drunk that he died alone but decided against it. He loved himself far too much to kill himself. His sense of loss had more to do with his ego and lowered status than with the missing woman. Their love was now like an untended garden in the snow. He tried to recall her beauty. He was worse at making decisions. Therefore, he had no big ideas on how to fix his life. Big sins lead to dead ends. He had been smart, but his mind was too simple to solve these types of problems.

Alexei Romovsky knew more of how to solve a problem. He knew of the mysterious departure of his former friend. He was saddened because he did not know where she was. After an encounter with Alexei, others noticed Sergei had several very dark bruises, scrapes, and a broken bone. He'd had to pay for his rebellion against some rules of society. Grief can turn violent, so the loss of the girl who had helped fix his marriage was a reason, in Alexei's way of thinking, for physical punishment. Besides, it had always been confusing to Alexei that her husband had not even considered a duel with the misguided lover who had stolen and ruined the treasured wife.

A lovely idea had formed in Natalia's healing mind. She pondered it a while before asking her husband's opinion of it. He did not understand it as well as his wife did. After several days of thought, he told her he approved. She was scared Constantine would think it was too forward. It took days for her husband to explain to her that he thought her question would be welcome to Constantine. Vladimir was not jealous of the attention his wife paid to others as long as she was faithful to him as a wife. She had never forgotten her wedding vows. Vladimir could not see God, but he could see his wife. His wife was enough of a Christ for him, so Vladimir felt God's spirit.

Vladimir had once asked his wife, "How can faith be infinite?"

She replied, "Because compassion is infinite." Her tone had been so logical. Her eyes were merry.

Natalia knew her husband liked her idea, so on one very cold day, she stood before Constantine. Looking at her face, Constantine reminded himself never to make the mistake of taking anything or anyone for granted. She asked Constantine if he felt it would be a good idea for her to be like a mother to his children, since no one knew if their real mother would return or if Constantine would remarry. She waited nervously and heard the words, "I accept."

Chapter 21
Desperate Letter

I did not lie to myself as much as you may think. What I have done was drastic. I lived in fear. You were not very sympathetic to fear. Some fears I could name. Some I could not. I am still afraid. I remember you so well. How well do you remember me? I am scared of being forgotten. Maybe it is my worst fear. My hatred grew stronger than my love. So, I made mistakes I only saw clearly later. What is too late? And who is the judge of that? I miss you. I miss him. I miss my children. Remember a time when you would not have doubted my word if I said I missed someone.

If I came back, what would you do? Is forgiveness stronger than sadness? Do you know all the reasons why I behaved as I did?

To leave my homeland affected me much more than I thought it would. How can a Russian live outside of Russia? My soul has lost the ability to change much.

Too much has changed for me to come back easily. Do you care if I come back?

The state Russia is in is too complicated and conflicted for people to care overmuch if one brokenhearted woman comes or goes. Must you care so much what others will think?

He lied so much.

Do you remember much of our wedding day and our arguments?

If you ask me to tell you more of myself, I will. If you ask me to tell you more of him, I will, for believe I have decided that he and I do not belong in the same room together. Why should I be loyal to him? If the soul has no one to be loyal to, does it die like a flower with no sun? Mine did.

If my children think of me, let them ask questions and answer them. They are my children and yours. Please, do not be without pity. Tell them of their mother. Do not let them be as confused as I am.

I do not need to ask you to keep him away from my children.

I make no threats.

I know my heart had to break too many times for me to see truths. This was very annoying to you. To me, this was not love. So, a poisonous love grew.

I beg for an answer.

I left without your forgiveness. Do you care if you have mine?

Constantine was bored with the letter. It was so odd that it was not signed. In disgust, he refused to reread it. It was as if reading it would make him feel dirty. She had been so weak to run away. Let her not come back. He was scared of what she might do. She seemed a little unhinged. What on Earth did she expect for an answer? It was hard to think of her again. He wasn't quite sure how she had gotten an unopened letter like this to him. She was in another country.

But people who had been rich were sometimes capable of strange things.

Chapter 22
Bitter Reply

I am not interested in his sentiments or yours. If you come back, do not expect a warm welcome from a man who has put the past behind him. Sour memories cancel out fond ones.

He is not a subject I wish to be written about any more than I want a repeating bad dream or for Russia to fall apart. Why do you write of him? The answer is not one I need.

I see by your letter you are not anymore fit to play the good parent than he is.

Love has caused many in history from the high to the low to make mistakes big and small. It does not need to be written, thought of, and acted on to the point of bothering me.

Our time together is over. It was your decision to trample on tradition, ritual, and religion. In light of this, your letter is crass. I am not sure why you wrote it. Your timing is terrible.

The loss of you is not something that makes the children suffer overmuch.

He sent this letter to her in hopes that she would just remain a bad memory. He did not want her influencing their offspring. So, he had kept his tone cool. He hoped she would not do anything rash in a rage. In his mind, she had not regained the ability to tell extreme behavior from more usual behavior. Good memories of her only made him feel worse. He didn't need the problem of her in his life while he worried about work, family, Russia, weather, trains, and any other thing he could think of to worry about.

He had been so shocked to get her letter.

Chapter 23
Second Desperate Letter

What do I call you? What is a home one cannot go back to?

When I left one man for another, I left one lifestyle for another. This has proved to be a mistake. I miss my children more than I miss you. Disturbing questions roam through my mind. Do you love others more than me? Do you hold anger against me? If I came back, would you take revenge? How fickle is fortune? Do you even care where I went? Is your wish to be a parent gone? When love grows cold, is it harder to remember what happened?

You will forget easier than I will. Your mind does not speak much to your heart. You can start a love you cannot keep. My rage does not replace the sorrow I feel. They both live together in me so that I cannot rest, see why I did what I did more clearly, or recover. I cry. Then I feel numb.

I see now you never fully saw what it would do to me to lose my place in society. You were not very interested in my children.

Love did not answer all the questions like I thought it would.

What did it do for you to treat me thus? I thought of you as a source of love. But now I see you were more of a gambler.

I lost the game. If I return, my life will never be the same. People will never forget. He will not take me back. You will probably refuse to see me. I remember your angry, cold, and changed face. My grief runs deep. Yours must be shallow.

Rest assured, I would stay away from you. Would you stay away from me?

Sergei was not excited to receive this letter. He had been forgetting details of her day after day. He did not think much about the letter. He did not care much about which country it had come from. His response to beauty was still so strong; he had been replacing sadness and memories of her with images and feelings he still enjoyed in his privileged lifestyle. He hated to be alone. He loved himself very much. However, he did not enjoy his own company.

Chapter 24
No Reply

Sergei did not answer her letter. He never considered it. He considered her rude to have sent it.

He wished he could get back to the military. But that was a mess he had made long ago. The Russian Army did not forget or forgive easily. He moved around between cities and the country. His mistakes, in his opinion, had not completely ruined his life. He resented that he was not considered to be as intimidating as he once was or as useful. His desires were almost the same as before. Desire ruled his life more than logic or pain. This put his mind in a frozen state late at night when he tried to fall asleep. He felt no need to discuss his troubles with others. If other people tried to bring it up in conversations, he curtly changed the subject. After a few weeks of this, something happened that shocked him very much. He began to feel lonely. He did not understand why. He had felt so strong. His mind had been able to reason so quickly on its own. But now his pride did not comfort him like it used to. What was this new emptiness? He didn't know what to do about it. It surprised him that he had trouble solving this problem. He had matched problems with solutions quickly in the past even if his thinking had been unusual. He had never paid much attention to loneliness in others. Without a complex example, he did not know many tricks to heal this new woe.

His nature was now cooler than hot.

Chapter 25
Mother's Letter

From a forlorn mother,

Does anything kind for me still linger in your hearts? Have my many mistakes made you all cold? Do you still suffer?

I have written him and your father.

I think of my children every day. But can I hope you return the favor? My nature does not give up hope easily. This can be good and this can be bad. I did not always know when to stop, listen, and learn.

I will not trouble you at length with how great my despair is. I will say I know little peace, and my soul longs for past joys.

Do you remember when I would show you certain things for the first time to answer your questions the way mothers do? I get tears in my eyes when I think on these things if am very tired and weary of being away. Do you know what to think of me?

Though I was intending to write much more, I have changed my mind. I am too wretched. I fear I will burden you with too much knowledge. I will not make that mistake again.

Know that I will never cease to think of my children.
What would it be like if I returned to you?
Your mother

Katerina's message received no reply.

79

Chapter 26
Children Left Behind

Katerina's letter imploring her son and daughter (the only other child was still too tiny to expect a message from) to pay attention to her filled that angry son and that sad daughter with confusion and offended pride. Her logic seemed a little disjointed to them. They talked heatedly about this together.

There were hot tears mostly shed by the girl. They spoke of their many opinions with their good friend Natalia. It helped keep all three minds from falling apart. The siblings talked to their father about the depressing message, too. Then, the brother and sister abruptly adopted a mindset that made it difficult to get them to talk about the letter at all.

The son had once had an aversion to drinking tea because when prepared for him before his teen years, several times the water had been too hot. This had turned the tea bitter. His irritation at the harsh taste now reminded him of the rotten feelings he had for his rejected mother. He tended to think on her very hard for hours or not at all for days because it hurt so much.

He did not have many friends. This did not bother him at all. His mind was too tired to be entertaining in front of others for very long. His love for his two siblings was especially sweet. However, he did not speak much of this affection. He had developed a hobby of learning history a little each day. He gained, among other opinions, the ideas that Jews might be the way they were because they moved around too many miles, that Alexander the Great (or awful) had suffered from manic depression the last two years of his life, that ancient Mesopotamia was probably an interesting place to live, and that the Duke of Monmouth had mostly been a selfish fool. The last man's messy execution in 1685 was, to the morbid Russian son, poetic justice for years of selfish behavior and compulsive lies. He had no idea how the Duke had soaked his head that much in Christianity and yet still had been so stupid. But he pitied Queen Anne Stuart because he saw she'd been lied about and slandered. It was not easy to get books on these subjects in Russia, but he was so high-class that it could be done.

The youngest child barely understood the mother was not around.

The other beloved sibling was a pensive, introverted, and delicate soul who feared dark secrets, deep water, and loved religion. She was also very curious. Her love of religion was so strong since her mother had left that her father had been worried, but he dropped his fears after realizing his daughter was not a fanatic to the point of harming herself, nor was she becoming mentally mature too fast. Most fathers he knew did not think this way, but he was no longer like most rich Russian fathers.

Chapter 27
Worried Father

Constantine knew the loss of the mother had affected his eldest child the most of all his children. He did not know why this was. Both his son and the father were talented at worrying. This made it hard for them to discuss troubles. They did not wish to make it worse for each other.

Sometimes it is hard to know if something is worth worrying about. It may be similar to how it is hard to tell if one is dreaming while the dream is still going on.

There is a way to not want a wife anymore, but there is no way to not desire a mother anymore.

Constantine kept in his mind a morbid idea his son had ever considered harming himself. The father also knew the son did not want to be followed all the time, made to feel stupid, or doubted. The son was very sensitive to criticism or hatred. He was willing to attend church. There, his eyes often had an intense, glazed expression. His mind did not wander though.

The father kept his son away from trains and close to people who felt emotions deeply but were not too aggressive. If the son was getting angry, his father tried to get into a conversation with him. The son was not weak-minded, but his feelings changed quickly. Twice his father saw him switch from tears to hot anger to confusion with numbness in under five minutes.

The son was sane, but Constantine made sure to get him to say aloud to his father that he had never considered harming himself since that dramatic day near the train. It was the truth. Constantine knew he was not being lied to.

Chapter 28
Confrontation

A black heart does not beat right for a long time; it may be a long time before a sinner repents.

Even though weeks had gone by, what some were afraid of (and others eagerly hoped for) finally happened.

Constantine accompanied his son to a ballet performance. He would never have let the troubled young teenager go alone. They trusted each other and were very aware of each other. They had distant looks in their eyes on this night. They were enjoying the performance even though dance was not usually what they chose for entertainment. They did not know dance was also the art that Sergei had chosen for entertainment this night. If the father and son had known Sergei would be there, they would not have come at all.

They noticed each other near the end of the performance. All three kept exchanging angry glances. The father feared what Sergei might do. He even doubted Sergei's sanity a bit.

Sergei still had elegance and intelligence, but he still had no moral magnetic pull to morals or sentimental beauty.

This was skillfully hidden by charm, training, and discipline.

The two people he was targeting tonight with insulting stares were not fooled. Others noticed and were very interested but tried not to be too obvious about it.

As people were leaving, Sergei began to follow Katerina's poor son, but he made sure to stay about twenty feet behind. The expression on his face was amused, cruel, cynical, and suave as he stared at the boy's back. The concerned father did not know why he was looking at the son instead of him.

Out on the street, in front of other people leaving the theater, Sergei said in a slightly loud voice, "It was a lovely performance for a saddened young man!" His voice sounded good, but it was full of sarcasm as sharp as a knife.

Constantine glanced at his worried son who had turned to face the idiot who had just spoken to him. Why did Sergei have to be so dramatic? Others were looking, looking away, and then looking back. They were unable to resist the temptation.

Then, Sergei disobeyed about one hundred social rules for high society in one moment by quickly grabbing the teenager's arm in a grip that almost hurt. The boy turned to look at him more quickly than Sergei had known he could. The boy wrenched himself free. He was angrier than scared. The energy in his tortured face was bright as the sun.

"Must you take peace away again from the son as you have from the mother? Why do you not lower your dignity further somewhere else?"

Sergei reached for him again, but the boy shocked him very much by punching him in the face. Many Russians had a streak of violence under nice manners, and elegance in Russia meant, among other things, a man could not offer mindless violence but could not accept insults like Sergei's. So, it was really a bit foolish for Sergei to be so shocked.

Whatever was left in Sergei's sordid soul that still looked noble showed on his face as he let the boy walk away, even though the older man still had not lost all the strength he had once had in the army. He refused to look at Constantine.

Chapter 29
Cynical Eyes

The tsar thought it all very funny, ridiculous, sad, and a little shocking. He did not know all of Constantine's little tragedy, but he did not wish to know. He heard bits and pieces here and there. It was more than enough. It had happened in and around royal courts, since God alone in His wisdom knew when. It was a mistake to care too much, about even former army men, who had lost control of their passions.

It was hard sometimes to decipher what was true and what wasn't. He was lied about with regularity even though he was a ruler. People were responsible for what they believed. Some of the lies about him and those around him were so silly. Women did not act anything like that. And why were the lies so often about women? So often in history, there were silly stories about women. Why did Russia have more than its fair share of them even though many Russians had a strong streak of common sense?

He felt his country needed stability more than many knew. There were so many problems; it was hard to remember them all and so much harder to do anything about it. Long ago, the nation had been formed of so many different peoples that now they still disagreed on much and still did not understand one another.

He lived in fear, so it was entertaining to alleviate some of the fear by hearing of some of the dramatic and/or stupid things the people around him did. He had seen many scoundrels and fools fit to try a saint's patience, but he did not know why Sergei did not gain wisdom.

Chapter 30
Gift

The little sister found out about the fight her brother had endured. She worried, cried, and prayed. Her intense piety was adorable in one so youthful. She used it to cope with her dreadful feelings, fears for her family and Russia, and her lack of direction she felt late at night. She had a long talk with her brother about the ugly episode after the ballet. She did not understand why Sergei broke so many rules.

In her emotional turmoil over the attack, she penned a gift for her brother. It took her days. She was also practicing in case she wrote something much longer as an adult. The gift was this:

King David

Assassin for God

King David was melodramatic, and this could be beautiful. But it also sometimes got the best of him and led to some deeply disturbing sins. He was the father of Solomon who was one of the wisest to ever live but who also fell into deep sin. Both men had one of the same problems after a while — treating women badly like they were worth no more than a chunk of dirt.

There is a very charming, pretty, and pure story of Solomon and the queen of Sheba in the Bible. It is about her search for wisdom. She traveled to see him and brought great gifts. She also gave hard questions which Solomon could answer. She was so impressed by his intelligence and wealth. This awe made her feel a sensation which might be called faint. Her reaction in the Bible is recorded in such a way that 'faint' may be a good modern word for it.

However, I do not think she was in distress.

Solomon made her gifts of anything she wished. She left.

There is an incorrect translation of the Bible that claims she said his wives must be so happy, but Solomon was not committing this sin at that time. The King James' Bible does not mention this remark of hers, and obviously adding it makes the whole story make no sense at all.

David, with his ability to form very close friendships, fit as a father of wise Solomon who could impress a queen to this extent.

I'm sure strict Jewish social rules also helped make David the successful killer and king that he was. David's personality was such that extreme love and extreme hate mingled often. Sometimes he behaved well at these times, but sometimes he gave in to temptation. He begged God for help and forgiveness, even though he spent a lot of his life as a very powerful and holy man. His lethal exploits against enemies made it clear he was one of the greatest warriors ever putting himself as a killer in the elite category that included Greek Alexander, Achilles, if he was real, and maybe ancient Britain's King Arthur such as he ever really existed.

David made many mistakes, but God forgave him again and again. David managed to die in the faith of his God.

A stroke of humor: David was one of the most difficult people to deal with ever – a passionate Jew.

In part of his mind, David was just a typical Jewish man. He was a younger son, a shepherd. He married and fathered kids. But he also had an extreme personality and expressed himself in a very dramatic fashion. He was often obsessed with his own reputation and wanting God to defend him from false accusations.

David's body must have endured a lot and been subject to great discipline. By the time it was getting near his death, he was having a problem with not having enough body heat. For medical purposes, to be near him and to keep him warm, a virgin girl was selected to be his companion. So, David had a pure heart when he allowed this girl to be recruited for him as a type of medical care. They wanted a girl who would not play silly games with bad morals around royalty. Besides, David was married.

When he sinned, David's heart went cold, and on the cross, Christ's heart stopped. But the love went on and on. King David had a strong will to fight. He faced danger many times. Sin, love, and sadness mingled in his life. He was a man of blood. The Lord blessed him with victory because David sought God with all his broken heart.

David was chosen by a great man of God to rise to a huge destiny. The Bible specifies David was handsome. It strongly hints he was not fully grown when he took on Goliath. Even though David was a strong person in body, it also took God's miracle power to destroy the extremely dangerous foe, Goliath.

David had a strong friendship with Jonathan, and they focused more on war and their friendship with each other than girls. This had something to do with David needing a very clean reputation in Israel because he carried such responsibility. He had already proved before Goliath's death that he could handle responsibility by taking care of his father's flocks of sheep even if a bear or big cat tried to steal one. The giant Goliath, a great champion of an army opposed to Israel, was no match for David's faith, and when David inflicted a severe head wound with a slingshot on this great enemy, even though Goliath owned stunningly powerful weapons, it was clear to the enemy David was a person almost unable to ever back down.

It was a while after being anointed as king by a man of God before David actually was king, thereby replacing Saul. Saul knew God, but several times he gave in to his evil nature. At first, he let David try to fight the Philistine on faith, but as David's stature grew in Israel due to his talent as a killer and victor, Saul eventually became infected with something that had destroyed kings, queens, families, friendships, relations between countries, and probably anything else you could think of: jealousy. He even tried unsuccessfully to put a spear through David. So, David would have known in no uncertain terms how Saul felt about him. These were two people with a part of their nature that was very direct and aggressive. But David had another side. Ironically, this ultraviolent killer with a bad temper liked harp music. He had talent as a musician himself and wrote song lyrics.

David suffered many blows to his pride. But the strength of his arm matched the speed of his mind. Fear was so strong; it drove him like an animal seeking shelter. Anger in the blood led to sin. God heard many lamentations begging for forgiveness. His love gave a purpose for living in David's life filled with many scenes of death. David often seemed quite hotheaded.

An episode showing his humility was endearing. When the idea was brought to him to perhaps become the king's son-in-law, he hesitated and specified it was not a frivolous thing to be in a king's family. But when he learned a fabulous military conquest was expected of him before he could marry the princess, he was well pleased at the prospect of marrying into the royal family.

David's son Solomon came from a marriage that never should have taken place. David had gotten another man's wife pregnant and then plotted the death of the husband. Unfortunately, this plot worked, and David wed the woman Bathsheba. The baby died. A later pregnancy of Bathsheba's produced Solomon.

When King David was earlier confronted by God's prophet about the king's sin with Bathsheba, the prophet at first behaved in a tricky fashion. He used symbolism so David did not realize he was condemning HIMSELF to death when he heard the tale from the prophet about an unfair man who, though he owned plenty of sheep, took a poor man's animal and made a feast of it. But during the same episode, the prophet revealed David was the guilty man and now David understood what was really being discussed: adultery and murder. David didn't die at this point. He did not have his own sentence carried out. God did not destroy him because he had displayed a sense of justice.

It was also prophesied the poor baby would die. So, the foolish David was not such a great man here in God's eyes. David could not even produce a sturdy child that would live long.

David's personality registered many emotions strongly, but he did not always display wisdom. He committed the serious sin of marrying and then, without divorcing, marrying another woman as well.

His desires sometimes overruled and overflowed his head, producing disastrous results. He needed to be a servant with a cool, wise voice to see and pierce to the heart of a matter. He needed reasoning to tell a blessing from a curse. David often displayed a strong sense of purpose. Even in his speech made towards the end of his life to his son Solomon, he got dramatic. The speech as a shortened version by me can be said to be: follow God, don't be a weak man, and be vengeful. All this emotion must've often exhausted David. Maybe what explained a lot of his behavior was the tiredness combined with the desert heat. Israel's king lifted up his helpless heart to God. Help was not near over and over, so God would have to intervene. Sin came and went, but love lasted and won in the end. David was such an energetic man that his son Solomon inherited peace even though David lived in such tough, hostile, and warlike times.

David went back and forth between blessings and curses in his life so often. I believe his sanity was a bit affected adversely several times. He did, in fact, pretend to be crazy once so an enemy king would be uninterested in him and leave him alone. The ploy worked. David was a very talented actor. David would've known much of insanity.

She gave it (written in her own handwriting) to him with some flowers, an icon, and a smile.

Chapter 31
Daughter's Journal

The same little girl had kept a diary ever since her mother had left the country. Most of it was in French. The rest was in Russian, which was harder for her to write in. She wrote of herself, of others she had seen (she thought this a bit sneaky), and a few in history because she knew her brother liked it. He liked it more than she did though. Some of her writing was real, and some of it was fantasy. Most of it was real.

In the first few weeks of suffering from a missing mother, the little miss had penned:

I do not understand why one lives with trash and throws away gold. Why do adults do it? And it's not to be spoken of. Well, at least not to those outside the house. I cannot think about it. Why leave a whole country? Why waste so much money? What a waste of a man, too! Some of the things adults say are so boring. I will try to write of something that interests me.

If ice is in the heart, it does not beat correctly. Like music with no sense of time played by a careless musician will do a troubled soul no good. Cold love in a hot heart leads to shame and grief. This kind of love comes when one loves an evil person just because they satisfy a selfish passion or enchant the eyes like a type of hypnosis.

Dangerous

I listen and hear nothing. I cannot recall all the clues. Is it my heart you use? Then take care, for it is stolen and therefore dangerous. Do I have yours? How does it work?

James

Bloom of youth and rare beauty became a twisted heart and mindless, crazed cruelty. Love looks like hate and hate looks like love in my world. I play games with people's minds, but too late I see I've played these games against me.

Anne and Mary were my brides, toys, enemies, and angels I feared and loved, but who really loves me?

They say I'm a fool and my love easily grows cool. I feel more than I think by feeling hate, memories, madness, and hurtful sanity.

What I loved most, I lost. I lost a crown and my heart finally went dead.

Many girls I was said to love, but love was just a mask on my face. My greatest love was not for a woman but a little girl: my last child by my last wife.

Trick Heart

My heart is like a trapdoor. My mind is like the moon — still and peaceful. My heart is like a mirror you cannot see and only I can read the feelings that flash there, caused by my face being drenched in tears.

Fall Turning into Winter

The leaves are falling and the snow will come.

My eyes hide my heart, and it's hard for me to read you.

You tried to keep your soul as a closed book.

Would you tell me how you felt with just one line and just one look? Or would you make me try and try to learn to love you?

I cannot try anymore. If you want me, you must try hard. Give it all you've got or completely fail.

Don't leave me alone.

I don't love you, but maybe I could if you can stop the nightmares and fill a crack in a heart.

The First

She was never born. She was just a miracle.

Before she felt sin's thorn, Eve heard a saintly call. It told her not to eat from a single tree. Its fruit would teach her more than she should know. Her innocent eyes would see too much, and disobedience would bring her low.

She failed the test. She had to be forgiven. Temptation will ruin the best. Love will no longer enliven the face looking down in disgrace. Eve had to leave the garden.

I saw one banished by their own sin. They abandoned all when shame crept in. They saw too late that it was a false game they could not win. Because they made the game's rules, they thought they would make others look like fools.

But they did not know they played a trick on themselves.

Black Garden

Long ago, he was a child in the dark brought into the light. It was a shock.

Sometimes he pleased. Sometimes he did not.

What he gave was not always what he got.

He fought and won. He gambled, and he won.

He had an angel's grace and a demon's anger.

There was a dark riddle and he was the answer.

He walked through a garden of black roses.

What?

What do you do when the poison is the cure? What do you decide when the sickness is the lure? It's another kind of temptation offering knowledge you do not need to know.

Roses and diamonds are forever if a memory in a heart is true. But what do you do if it lies and causes brokenhearted lover's sighs? What if forever turns to never?

Roses are soft, and diamonds are hard. Your tricky eyes are soft, but your heart is hard.

If a desire too strong creeps in, what it takes to stop a bad habit is what the desire stole.

I need to see you. I never saw you again.

The other half of my heart still rests in someone I care for. Roses wilt. Wine wears off.

Your memory is burned in my mind like letters of gold on an invitation. You loved me once. Will you ever love me again?

Evergreen

I have loved you long, and I have loved you dearly. Have I ever known all your heart? Have I ever cured your fear?

Evergreen trees give life on and on as I love you on and on. I could not refrain from tears if you were gone. I can see deeply in you because I adore you.

Love's evergreen power fades my darkest moods. Your eyes control my heart. If your love can heal, it can tear apart.

I bargain with God when beauty deceived when it should have blessed.

What is the price of the evergreen tree?

She was too shy to show the journal to anyone. She was apprehensive people might criticize it. She did not take criticism well.

Chapter 32
Daughter's Request

One day, that same little girl, after much thought, presented her father with a list. He had not known she was going to do it. It was a long-pondered list of things she wanted.

1. *A visit to the country*
2. *Chocolate*
3. *To learn to knit*
4. *To know if Sergei had suddenly left the country, too*
5. *Books*
6. *To be allowed to give a pet name to her younger sibling*
7. *Singing lessons (if possible)*
8. *To see the letter her mother had sent her father*

Her father smiled when seeing the list for the first time.
"What? No rubles?"
She tried to be funny in her sorrow.
"What? Should I have asked to learn to gamble?"

Her father had a long talk with Natalia about the last request on the list. Then, he let the little girl see the letter. He hoped it would not lead to regret.

Chapter 33
Sister's Prayer

This was whispered in a church.

"I cannot always withstand the pain. Sin's stain is poisoning my life even if the sin is not mine. It is not fair.

"Help my brother more than me. He considered going back to You too early and is too young to die. Be near.

"Let people who planted good seed get good fruit, and let the blind reap bad crops. For some sins, people pay for the rest of their lives.

"What purpose is there to life? It is hard to see a plan in all the confusion.

"If a person loves, why must they choose to be so distant?

"Lead away from tears and disgrace. Be strength where there is no strength.

"It is hard to bring the proud and powerful low if they disobey holy commandments. Give justice. Watch over my country, my brother, those who have faith, those who are faithful, and me."

She hoped no other people had overheard her clearly.

Chapter 34
Gossip

The talk went on and on. It was taking people an unusually long time to lose interest in this subject. It was uttered by people telling the truth, by liars, by bored people, and people who wanted a reaction.

"He left her."

"No, she left him."

"She died of a serious illness that lasted weeks."

"No, I heard she threatened to kill herself after getting a scathing message from the last man she left. But someone managed to restrain her."

"That is so stupid. Where did you hear that? And if it is true, why do you not know who restrained her?"

"He has been drunk way too often. He misses the military more than any woman."

"He would never drink so much that it would destroy his handsome face. I do not believe you."

"She will never come back. She told me so."

"She told you nothing. And who cares if she ever comes back? I certainly do not, I am so glad she left. She was so depressing to look at. I pity the children though. It would have been worse for them if she had stayed."

"You may be right. You are wrong about almost everything else though!"

"It was so uninteresting in the end. All she wanted to do before she left was love him, and I hate people like that. I do not like those with only one great goal in life because they often ignore those around them. They are often disrespectful to their superiors, too."

"She did not have a noble thought in her head."

"Oh, she used to. It is just that love makes people seem stupid. He lowered her. He did it on purpose. Someone like that uses people up, and then he is gone or hates them. He was so shallow, but most did not notice it because he was so handsome and used a lot of flattery and philosophy. I could not stand to be in a conversation with him for two minutes. I go back and forth between great anger at the whole situation and not caring one bit. They became like dessert; there was no dinner. By which I mean, they were not whole people. I pity people like that, but I do not really care what happens to them. It is not a compassionate type of pity. It annoys me."

"It's a pity they are both still alive. What ever happened to duels?"

"That man's ego could certainly make someone want to kill themselves. I wonder if she did."

"Probably not. My best guess is she was not in love any longer."

"People like that desire pity but do not deserve it any more than a dog does."

"What kind of idiot leaves a woman like that?"

"What kind of idiot takes a woman like that in the first place?"

"If she comes back, I will have no wish to speak to her as long as she lives. I would have no idea what to say. There are not many social rules to tell one what to say in a case like that."

"I hear the baby is doing nicely."

"There is always something good even in the middle of a situation with so many bad qualities."

"What is he doing?"

"Nothing."

"What do you mean nothing? He's got to be doing something. He once had so much energy. It is such a shame they did not contribute more to society. Instead, they decided to set a bad example. I blame him more than her."

"Was it his idea or hers to wreck their lives? Who started it?"

"Stop being silly."

"I am not silly. From what I have seen, this sort of thing is often the man's idea at first. The woman is then stupid enough to listen to him."

"She listened to almost no one but him near the end. That was what was wrong with her. The loss of the children will affect her for the rest of her life. I do not know how their father sees it though."

"He is even angrier than the children. That kind of man never cools off."

"That is not true. Children feel a mother's loss even if they hate their mother. I hope she cannot use that feeling to lie her way back into their lives. God forbids."

"She came back in secret. She has been in Russia for the past few weeks. She has lost her sanity though."

"That is not true. Of all the stupid rumors I have heard about this mess, that is one of the most unrealistic. She is too ashamed to come back."

"She is too much of a fool to come back. Russia was the only home she ever knew. A woman like that can only fit in Russia. She no longer sees where she belongs. If she comes back, she will listen to no one's advice. She will be too obstinate to be a good friend."

"She was not like that before. He was obstinate, and it made her so. He changed her so much. He made her think it was her idea."

"I wonder if she has begun to look old."

"He will not take her back if she has."

"He will not take her back if she is lovely or not. He is afraid of her now."

"He is not. You are too dramatic. You made that lie up yourself. The lies you hear from others are better. Stick with those."

"He is in love with someone else."

"No, he is not."

"Someone else is in love with him."

"No, she is not."

Katerina was not dead, but there were not a lot of people who cared. Her value to the nation was just not high enough.

She was also still abroad.

Chapter 35
Opera Is the Cure

They were going to the opera, and none of these three people cared much which one it was as long as it was not awful. Constantine was going with his oldest child, but it was unusual that he was also going with his next child. None of them felt very keen about opera in general, but this time, they all sought to lift their spirits by the singing. It was a lovely chance to replace bad memories and hopefully fix them.

They were not afraid of seeing Sergei because they knew he would not repeat an ugly scene or use violence in front of the daughter. They did not even look for him.

The usher was civil. The chandeliers looked like jewelry that a kind fairy had invented. The little girl looked just as much at the theater and the people in it as she looked at the singer and her jewels. The child tried to put into her memory as much as she could.

Chapter 36
Constantine's Revenge

It was easier to do than he had expected. He did not know why. At first, he wondered if he should even do it. Would it cost Russia dearly? But how could he just accept the way he had been treated. It was impossible. What would others think? Katerina had made the mistake of not caring what others thought. He was scared for his job and the way he would be looked at for the rest of his life. A duel was rather late, and not an idea he intended to take seriously. His contempt for this man was too strong. It would make for excited gossip, but he had never cared much for gossip about violence.

He knew Sergei had cared more than he would have liked to admit about his place in the army. He knew Sergei toyed constantly with the idea of getting it back. It was not information that was easy to get, but it was information that was hard to get because Sergei was so useful. Sergei hated a life with no focus. It took intelligent, forceful talk to the right people including at least two regimental commanders, six nobles, and their talk to the tsar himself. It also took promises of loyalty and agreement to back some of their ideas about Russia and money. These promises would not have worked without his reputation for hard work. But he got what he wanted; he kept Sergei out of the army.

When Sergei found out why his goals came to nothing, he was livid with rage. But he also wondered why it had taken so long for this man to make a drastic action.

Chapter 37
Sergei's Opinion of Russia

"Don't you dare kill yourself in front of me!" He woke up from the dream after it had given him this line in a female voice. It had a slight echo, and it had been hard to tell if it had been a woman's voice or a child's. He knew his life in this country had taken on the quality of being a little like a bad dream in that it was hard to distinguish reality from lies. The female voice had not even sounded very upset. Did it mean suicide was acceptable if she could not see it? What did it mean?

Sergei tried to get out of the dream's mood by thinking of his life in Russia as it was now. He must try to think what to do.

Russia seemed to him to be changing so fast. It was not good. These people, for the most part, were not as smart as he was. It was his morals that were stupid. He saw other people's sins more clearly than he saw his own. At least change was not boring. Almost anything was better than being bored. And some nobles did the most awful things when they were bored. Sometimes they even did these bad things because someone ELSE was bored. It was a pattern in history. He saw that poverty was a dead end with Russia's winters. So many of his fellow countrymen's minds were tired. This led to a mindset like cranky children. Many bad ones pretended to be more mature than they were and pretended to have political views. So, they fought and came up with bad ideas that they tried to set in motion very quickly. They wanted fast answers to try to find rest. They did not see that some of the questions had simple answers. Much respect was lacking. But many in the lower classes were in the wrong in that they thought the way to fix a problem was to have even less respect. There were so many bad ideas that people who had once looked for ways to solve a problem were jaded and no longer noticed a good idea when they heard one. Most people cared, but too many cared about the wrong things. Decay had been spreading a long time. He did not think the country would end. In his arrogance, he felt he could assume different attitudes that were not real to get what he wanted with ease in his homeland. He had known great sadness, so he understood the suffering of others more than people knew because he did not express it.

Chapter 38
Vladimir's Opinion of Russia

He felt unqualified to have too many opinions about Russia. Some were so religious, and some were not religious at all. He saw there were so many groups that their differences made it hard for them to get along. They did not wish to know about one another or understand one another. It was very sad. There were a lot of liars in Russia. His mind did not understand or process lies very well, so he often felt left behind. This did not bother him much. He did not find lies very interesting. Russia was in a more delicate state than some knew, but a bigger problem was not being willing to act to save it. This inertia had been a problem in Russia for centuries. There could be no cheating with a false cure this time.

The Slavic nature was dramatic, so it kept one from being bored, but it also liked to fight too much when an individual did not have a decent outlet for anger. Russia kept trying to change, but a lot of Slavs did not do well with change.

Why did Russia keep eating itself in a similar way to the French Revolution? It was a terrible habit. Cruelty was seen as a means to an end, but a plan like that is always flawed and can get further out of control. It can do even more damage than the planner wanted it to.

So much of Russia was beautiful that he would have hated to see it all destroyed. The people's strong interest in art should have been indulged more.

The unhappy citizens did not always think it was important to find long-term solutions. But when happiness ran out, they got upset. It was hard to know who to blame.

So many thought doubts were the answer. They did not see doubt would rot everything. Doubt was the opposite of hope.

Maybe it was the Viking blood that made people do crazy things.

So long ago in this country, the people had been nomads. Was this part of the problem? Now, could they not work together or settle down.

There was an appreciation for power. Its success had been displayed again and again for centuries.

There was another appreciation for royalty precisely because so much of the history was so primitive. And those who did not wish to be elegant still liked to observe elegance.

One thing Vladimir did not understand was why Russia had reached out to other countries to be influenced by them long ago but now did not seem to want to do that.

There was an obsession with strength, but some strengths fail without warning.

There were ways for love to survive in Russia, but for centuries, they had been too mysteriously hard to find if hidden by bad social rules.

Some of the rulers of the past usually tended to be very strong or very unstable or both. Some of them used war too often. What on Earth was wrong with peace?

Of course, there was some poverty. However, the answer to that was obvious.

Vladimir saw his country as a place where he must relate with proper etiquette to many types of people whether he understood them or not. If he did not, he felt he would be rude.

Chapter 39
Sinner Tries to Make a Decision

His mind flitted from one thought to the next. He could not always control his moods. He had not decided on any firm course of life for weeks. Finally, all of this became a state of mind he could bear no longer. He knew he should have seen it would happen. It was as if he had no guiding star.

He decided he needed something or someone to love very much. When she had left the country, he had not missed her much. Memories of little things were continuously fading. He did not recall so well the slight smile on her face, the peculiar light in her eyes as she thought of leaving her husband and children, or the hatred in the same pretty eyes as she narrowed them at him even though she had abandoned family, religion, and status for him.

As empty days wore on, he got into fights (some of them were physical), visited some of the right people and some of the wrong people, got drunk, and got sick of it. He was tired of seeing the bows on dresses of women who could not learn to walk gracefully in high heels. He was tired of the face powder on faces of silly women that talked of silly things. His heart could not respond even when there was beauty in life. The fist fights (he never started them) were with men he used to see when Sergei lived in military camp, who tended to start stupid arguments.

He started to read more. At first, it was bad novels. But then he knew that would not do the trick. A friend he had known for a long time suggested some history to teach lessons to solve the problems.

"The human race has made every mistake it can possibly make. All you have to do is read history books to learn what not to do." The friend's quote was their own, and they passed it on to Sergei with pride. They got him several works on people of the past, including tyrants, princesses, martyrs, and a short-lived king. It was a lot of information, but it was going to take a lot of information to fix his life.

Sergei tried to concentrate on it all, but his ability to focus faded and returned again and again. He tried to deduce reason from bad judgment.

He thought, *Russian rulers were too violent. No, not always. They had to keep control. That English queen made a fool of herself. She burned so many because her father was cruel to her. She just claimed it was because she was Catholic. This is when people try to look good and only make themselves look worse.*

He tried to concentrate on a bit of one work that explained the king that died so soon. A friend bet him money that he could not read the whole thing without stopping because he had become so flighty. He read only forty pages of a work on Alexander the Great that explained folly, despair, and bad judgment plus genius. It was hard to tell them apart.

That was about as long as he could concentrate. He stopped thinking about this abruptly. It horrified him too much and made him too sad. After reading the work on Alexander, he knew his affair with another man's wife would not have lasted even if she had wanted it to. He decided he needed to shock someone. He decided to send his own message.

Chapter 40
Too Much Coffee

He thought too much about the old queen ordering all those Protestants burned. Then, he began drinking too much coffee. So, it was her fault. He was not an addict. He liked it hot and cold.

He decided people who had contempt for religion were too proud and missing something. He was not devout. It just made sense to him that faith had lasted for centuries for a reason. He had known men whose sense could not last one night.

He was not in love, but he missed an idea of a girl from months ago. It seemed longer ago than it was. The feelings were mixed up. He used to be more logical. He needed to accomplish something big. Some thought he had no soul, but he knew he did because it tried to find answers when he could not sleep.

The coffee made him seem foolishly proud even if it was really that he was unsure. It also made him angry. He was disgusted.

He yelled to an acquaintance, "I am drinking so much coffee and not getting drunk. If I was stronger, it would be alcohol that would be my downfall! I am not a man!"

They laughed and shook their head.

Chapter 41
Trusted Hand

Sergei wrote a letter to Natalia that stated some reasons why he had acted as he had and said he wondered what might have been. It was made politely clear he did not want her. His tone was cool. To show good faith such as he understood it, he sent it to her husband to read and show it to her. He made sure a very trusted servant took it to him.

So, dearest reader, this is the tale I have created, and I will stop writing soon. I hope it has instructed your heart and morals or at least made you feel a little better.

THE END